AI for Emo Influencers

AI for Emo Influencers

Matthew Petchinsky

1

AI for Emo Influencers: Growing an Online Following Without the Anxiety

By: Matthew Petchinsky

AI & RESPONSIBILITY DISCLAIMER

This book, *Emo Influencers: Growing an Online Following Without the Anxiety*, was created with the assistance of artificial intelligence (AI) tools used as a supportive writing aid. AI technology was utilized to help organize ideas, refine language, explore creative concepts, and assist in drafting content. All final decisions regarding structure, tone, themes, interpretation, and presentation were guided, reviewed, and curated by the author.

This work is intended for **informational, educational, and inspirational purposes only**. It does **not** constitute medical advice, psychological counseling, psychiatric treatment, or professional mental health care. The content within this book should not be used as a substitute for therapy, diagnosis, or treatment provided by licensed mental health professionals. If you are experiencing severe anxiety, depression, panic attacks, emotional distress, or thoughts of self-harm, please seek immediate help from a qualified professional or a trusted support resource.

The experiences, strategies, reflections, and perspectives shared in this book are **generalized frameworks**, not personalized prescriptions. Emotional responses to online visibility, social media engagement, creative exposure, and public interaction vary greatly from person to person. What may feel empowering or calming for one individual may feel overwhelming or triggering for another. Readers are encouraged to move at their own pace, honor their emotional boundaries, and adapt or disregard any practices that do not feel safe or appropriate for them.

This book does not promise, guarantee, or imply specific outcomes related to follower growth, audience size, financial success, social validation, or emotional well-being. Online platforms, algorithms, cultural trends, and audience behavior are constantly changing and remain outside the author's or AI's control. Any references to growth, visibility, or influence are illustrative rather than predictive.

The author and publisher assume no responsibility for any emotional, psychological, financial, reputational, or personal outcomes that may arise from the use or interpretation of the material in this book. By choosing to read this work, you acknowledge that you are solely responsible for how you apply—or choose not to apply—the ideas presented.

This book intentionally approaches anxiety, emotional sensitivity, and creative identity from a **non-clinical, non-diagnostic perspective**, emphasizing self-reflection, emotional awareness, and creative agency rather than pathology. It is not designed to label, define, or medically interpret emotional states.

Any mention of platforms, tools, strategies, or online behaviors is provided for illustrative and educational purposes only and does not constitute endorsement, affiliation, or professional recommendation. The inclusion of AI-assisted content does not imply automation of influence, emotional manipulation, or guaranteed engagement.

This work respects emotional vulnerability, neurodivergence, creative sensitivity, and personal autonomy. Readers are encouraged to prioritize their well-being over metrics, visibility, or external validation. Taking breaks, disengaging, or choosing privacy over exposure are all valid outcomes.

By continuing to read this book, you acknowledge and accept this disclaimer in full.

Introduction

Let AI Handle Social Media While You Stay Mysterious

There was a time when mystery was power.

Before algorithms demanded constant visibility.
Before creators were expected to explain themselves daily.
Before silence was interpreted as failure.

In emo culture, mystery was never a flaw—it was the language. Shadowed profiles. Half-spoken truths. Lyrics that meant everything without explaining anything. Presence without overexposure. Feeling without performance.

But modern social media was not built for that.

Today's platforms reward noise, frequency, relentless access, and emotional labor disguised as "authenticity." You're expected to post even when you're exhausted. To show your face even when you don't feel like yourself. To perform vulnerability on demand. To turn your inner world into consumable content.

For emotionally sensitive creators, introverts, neurodivergent minds, anxious artists, and those drawn to the emo aesthetic—not just as fashion but as identity—this system can feel suffocating.

This book exists because **you don't need to burn yourself alive to be seen.**

You don't need to overshare.
You don't need to explain your pain.
You don't need to be constantly available.

And you certainly don't need to sacrifice your nervous system for an algorithm.

Artificial intelligence changes the rules.

Not by making you louder—but by letting you be quieter.

AI offers a way to **separate presence from exposure**, **output from exhaustion**, **growth from anxiety**. It allows your ideas, aesthetics, and creative signals to exist online without demanding that *you* constantly perform. It can handle structure, scheduling, captions, drafts, pattern recognition, and repetition—so you can remain partially unseen, partially protected, and fully yourself.

This book is not about becoming a hyper-visible influencer.

It is about becoming a **controlled signal**.

A presence that feels intentional instead of desperate.
A digital footprint that feels curated instead of invasive.
An online identity that does not devour the person behind it.

"Mysterious" does not mean fake.
It does not mean cold.
It means **selective**.

It means deciding what stays private.
It means letting your work speak when you don't want to.
It means building an audience that resonates with your energy—not demands access to your life.

Inside these pages, you will learn how to:

- Use AI as a **buffer**, not a replacement for your humanity
- Create content without emotional overexertion
- Maintain aesthetic consistency without constant effort
- Grow quietly, steadily, and sustainably
- Protect your inner world while still being discoverable

This is not a guide to "beating" social media.

It's a guide to **coexisting with it on your terms**.

You are allowed to log off.
You are allowed to disappear between posts.
You are allowed to let silence be part of your brand.

The emo influencer was never meant to shout.

They were meant to haunt timelines.
To linger.
To be felt more than explained.
Let AI handle the noise.
You stay mysterious.

Chapter 1: AI Content Creation for Instagram, TikTok, and YouTube

Separating Your Presence from Your Energy

Social media platforms are built to collapse the distance between creator and audience. They reward immediacy, visibility, and constant output, often at the expense of emotional safety. For emo creators and influencers, this can feel like being permanently exposed—always watched, always interpreted, always expected to perform a version of yourself that may not exist on a given day. AI introduces a crucial separation: your presence online no longer has to be fueled by your moment-to-moment emotional energy.

When AI assists with content creation, your nervous system is no longer the primary engine of your brand. Instead of posting only when you feel emotionally "ready," you can create systems that allow your ideas, aesthetics, and values to flow consistently—even during low-energy or withdrawn periods. This is not detachment; it is preservation. You remain emotionally intact while your presence remains active.

Instagram, TikTok, and YouTube each demand different forms of output, but none of them require you to be emotionally available at all times. AI can help you batch captions, outline scripts, generate posting schedules, and suggest visual concepts without pulling you into the exhausting loop of constant decision-making. You choose when to engage deeply and when to step back.

This separation also reduces anxiety around visibility. When your content is prepared in advance or generated through a collaborative AI process, posting no longer feels like an emotional cliff. You are not asking, "How do I feel today?" before showing up. You are simply executing a plan that already aligns with your identity.

Ultimately, this shift reframes social media from a place of emotional extraction into a controlled interface. You are no longer pouring yourself into the feed. You are curating a signal—one that reflects you without consuming you.

Using AI to Translate Mood into Content

Emo expression has always relied on mood rather than explanation. A look, a lyric, a shadowed image—these communicate far more than explicit storytelling ever could. AI excels at translating abstract emotional states into structured content without requiring you to verbalize or justify them. This makes it a powerful ally for creators who feel deeply but speak selectively.

Instead of asking yourself, "What should I post today?", you can start with "What does today feel like?" AI can take simple emotional descriptors—numb, heavy, distant, longing, static—and turn them into captions, hashtags, short-form scripts, or visual prompts. This removes the pressure to perform emotional clarity when all you have is a feeling.

On Instagram, this might mean AI-generated captions that carry poetic ambiguity rather than direct messaging. On TikTok, it might look like moody voiceover scripts or text overlays that hint rather than explain. On YouTube, AI can help you outline reflective, atmospheric videos without forcing high-energy performance or constant talking.

This approach allows your content to remain emotionally authentic without being emotionally draining. You are not overexposing your inner life—you are allowing it to echo. AI acts as a translator, not a confessor.

By letting AI handle the articulation, you preserve the rawness of your emotions while avoiding burnout. Your audience receives something resonant, and you remain protected behind the veil of creative distance.

Platform-Specific AI Strategies Without Overexposure

Each major platform has its own rhythm, expectations, and psychological pressure points. Instagram prioritizes visual consistency and caption tone. TikTok favors repetition, trend-awareness, and short emotional hooks. YouTube rewards structure, pacing, and longer-form engagement. AI can help you meet these requirements without forcing you to fragment yourself across platforms.

For Instagram, AI can generate caption banks that match your aesthetic—short, poetic, ambiguous, or emotionally restrained. You can reuse variations without sounding repetitive, allowing your feed to feel cohesive rather than chaotic. This minimizes the emotional labor of constantly "finding the right words."

On TikTok, AI can help you repurpose the same emotional concept into multiple formats: text-on-screen, voiceover, or silent visuals paired with music. You do not need to chase trends aggressively; AI can adapt your core themes to current formats without diluting your identity.

For YouTube, AI excels at outlining scripts, structuring reflective content, and pacing videos so you don't have to improvise on camera. This is especially valuable if speaking feels vulnerable or draining. You can record calmly, knowing the structure already exists.

The key is not to let platforms dictate your emotional availability. AI allows you to meet technical demands while staying emotionally selective. You are present everywhere—but exposed nowhere.

Batching Content as an Act of Emotional Self-Defense

One of the most powerful uses of AI is content batching. Instead of creating under pressure, you create in contained, intentional sessions. This is especially important for creators who experience anxiety spikes around posting, engagement, or audience reaction.

With AI, you can generate weeks—or even months—of captions, video outlines, and posting ideas in a single session. This removes the daily emotional decision-making that often leads to avoidance or burnout. You are no longer asking yourself to be creative on demand.

Batching also creates psychological safety. When content is prepared ahead of time, posting becomes mechanical rather than emotional. You are executing a plan, not exposing yourself. This is crucial for maintaining consistency without sacrificing mental health.

AI helps ensure that batched content still feels varied and intentional. It can rewrite, remix, and reframe ideas so they don't feel stale or robotic. You remain the curator; AI handles the repetition.

Over time, batching transforms social media from a constant drain into a background system. Your creative energy is preserved for moments that matter, rather than being consumed by algorithms.

Maintaining Mystery Through Controlled Disclosure

Mystery is not created by saying nothing—it is created by choosing what not to say. AI can help you maintain this balance by shaping content that hints, suggests, and evokes without revealing too much. This is especially aligned with emo aesthetics, where restraint often speaks louder than confession.

Instead of oversharing personal details, AI can help you frame experiences in symbolic or universal language. Pain becomes atmosphere. Growth becomes implication. Your audience feels something without being invited into every corner of your life.

On visual platforms, AI can suggest imagery, lighting, and color palettes that reinforce mood without explanation. On text-based content, it can generate captions that feel intimate without being invasive.

This controlled disclosure protects your boundaries while deepening audience connection. People lean in when not everything is explained. AI helps you craft that tension intentionally rather than accidentally oversharing.

Mystery becomes a strategy, not a defense mechanism. You are no longer hiding—you are choosing.

Building a Sustainable AI-Assisted Creative Loop

The goal of AI content creation is not automation—it is sustainability. A healthy creative loop includes ideation, creation, rest, and reflection. AI supports each phase without replacing your humanity.

You ideate by feeding AI moods, themes, and boundaries.
You create by selecting what resonates and discarding what doesn't.
You rest while scheduled content posts without your involvement.
You reflect without pressure to immediately produce more.

This loop prevents the emotional whiplash that many creators experience. You are not constantly reacting to metrics or audience feedback. You are operating from a grounded, intentional place.

Over time, this approach builds trust—with yourself first, and then with your audience. Your content feels steady, atmospheric, and authentic because it is not being created under emotional duress.

AI does not make you less human. Used correctly, it gives your humanity room to breathe.

Exercises

Exercise 1: Mood-to-Content Translation

1. Write down three emotional states you experience often.
2. For each emotion, list three words or images associated with it.
3. Use AI to generate one caption, one short video idea, and one long-form video outline for each emotion.
4. Review the outputs and remove anything that feels too revealing.
5. Save the rest for future use.

Exercise 2: Platform Boundary Mapping

1. List what you are comfortable sharing on Instagram, TikTok, and YouTube separately.
2. Identify one boundary you do not want crossed on each platform.
3. Use AI to rewrite existing content so it respects those boundaries.
4. Create a short guideline you can reuse for future prompts.

Exercise 3: One-Week Batch Session

1. Choose a single mood or theme for the week.
2. Ask AI to generate seven captions or scripts around that theme.
3. Edit only for tone, not perfection.
4. Schedule the content.
5. Log off once it's done.

Journal Prompts

1. What parts of social media drain me the most emotionally?
2. Where do I confuse visibility with obligation?
3. How does mystery feel safer than explanation for me?
4. What would change if my content didn't require my daily presence?
5. What emotions do I want my audience to *feel*, not know?
6. Where do I overshare out of fear rather than choice?
7. How does batching content change my anxiety levels?
8. What boundaries feel non-negotiable for my online identity?
9. How can AI support me without replacing my voice?
10. What would sustainable creativity look like in my life?

Closing Reflection

You were never meant to be consumed by the platforms you use. Your creativity does not owe constant access, constant explanation, or constant availability. AI offers a way to protect your inner world while still allowing your work to exist, circulate, and connect.

When you let systems carry the weight, you reclaim your emotional autonomy. When you choose mystery, you choose longevity. This chapter is not about doing more—it is about **being intact while doing enough**.

Let the machine handle the mechanics.

You keep your soul.

Chapter 2: Emo Blog Automation – Writing Posts with Zero Effort

Why Blogs Still Matter for Emo Creators

Long before short-form video and endless scrolling, blogs were sanctuaries. They were quiet places where emotion could stretch out, where thoughts didn't have to be condensed into fifteen seconds, and where readers arrived intentionally rather than by accident. For emo creators, blogs still offer something social media cannot: space without performance.

Blogs do not demand your face, your voice, or your immediate availability. They allow you to exist in written form, which is often safer for those who process feelings internally or slowly. The problem is not blogging—it is the *effort* blogging seems to require. Sitting down, organizing thoughts, editing, formatting, and publishing can feel overwhelming, especially when energy is low.

This is where automation changes everything. AI allows you to create blog content without entering a high-effort emotional state. You no longer need to wait for inspiration or clarity. You can begin with fragments—phrases, moods, or questions—and let AI shape them into complete posts.

For emo influencers, this restores blogging to its original purpose: expression without pressure. You are not chasing virality. You are building a quiet archive of presence that grows over time, supports discoverability, and never demands emotional urgency.

Automation does not cheapen the work. It simply removes friction between what you feel and what gets published.

Turning Feelings into Finished Posts Automatically

Many creators believe writing requires full emotional immersion. In reality, that belief is what makes writing exhausting. AI allows you to externalize the heavy lifting—structure, coherence, transitions—while you remain emotionally neutral or protected.

You can start a blog post with a single sentence, a lyric-like line, or a question that has been looping in your head. AI can expand that fragment into an introduction, develop body sections, and suggest a closing reflection that aligns with your tone. You do not need to "explain yourself" for this to work.

This process is especially powerful for emo-styled blogging, where ambiguity and mood are strengths rather than weaknesses. AI can help you maintain that tone consistently, even across dozens of posts, without you having to relive the emotion each time.

The key is intention. You decide the emotional range you are willing to express. AI fills in the gaps without pushing beyond your boundaries. You remain the editor, not the confessor.

Writing becomes less about effort and more about permission—permission to be incomplete and still publish.

Creating an Automated Emo Blog System

Automation works best when it becomes a system rather than a one-off tool. An automated emo blog system does not require daily attention. It functions quietly in the background, much like your creative presence itself.

The system begins with themes: isolation, resilience, nostalgia, quiet anger, emotional recovery, creative withdrawal. These themes can be stored and reused. AI can generate multiple posts per theme without repeating itself, allowing your blog to feel expansive without being overwhelming.

Next comes scheduling. Posts can be generated in batches and scheduled weeks or months in advance. This removes the emotional weight of "needing to write" on any given day. Your blog grows even when you are resting.

Finally, automation supports consistency without urgency. You are no longer tied to productivity cycles. The blog becomes a slow-burn artifact rather than a performance.

This system allows you to show up without showing *everything*.

Zero-Effort SEO Without Selling Your Soul

SEO often feels clinical, mechanical, and incompatible with emo aesthetics. But visibility does not have to erase mood. AI can quietly optimize your blog posts for discoverability while preserving your voice.

You do not need to stuff keywords or flatten your language. AI can weave relevant phrases naturally into your writing without making it sound commercial or hollow. This allows your posts to be found by people who are already searching for what you are expressing.

SEO automation also reduces anxiety around "being seen." You are not promoting aggressively. You are simply allowing your work to be discoverable over time. This is a gentler form of growth.

The result is a blog that feels intimate yet accessible. Your words remain yours. AI handles the mechanics of visibility.

You stay honest. The system stays functional.

Protecting Emotional Boundaries Through Written Distance

Writing can feel safer than speaking—but it can also become a trap if you overshare. AI helps maintain distance by reframing personal experiences into reflective or symbolic language. You are not exposing wounds; you are shaping atmosphere.

This distance is crucial for sustainability. Readers connect with themes, not details. They feel understood without needing access to your life. AI assists in maintaining that balance consistently.

By using AI to rewrite drafts with less specificity, you protect your privacy while keeping emotional depth intact. This prevents regret, vulnerability hangovers, or the feeling that you've shared too much.

Boundaries are not walls. They are filters. Automation helps you maintain them without constant vigilance.

Letting Your Blog Work While You Rest

The ultimate promise of automation is rest. A blog that updates itself allows you to step away without disappearing. Your voice remains present even when you are not.

This is especially important for creators who experience burnout cycles, anxiety, or emotional shutdowns. You do not need to announce breaks or justify silence. The system continues quietly.

Over time, this creates a sense of stability—for both you and your audience. Your blog becomes a steady pulse rather than a sporadic outpouring.

Rest is not a failure. It is part of the system.

Exercises

Exercise 1: Fragment to Post

1. Write three unfinished thoughts or emotional fragments.
2. Feed each fragment to AI with a tone request (moody, reflective, restrained).
3. Generate full blog posts.
4. Edit only for comfort, not perfection.
5. Save for future scheduling.

Exercise 2: Theme Bank Creation

1. List ten recurring emotional themes in your life.
2. Ask AI to generate five blog ideas per theme.
3. Select only the ones that feel safe to publish.
4. Store them as a reusable content bank.

Exercise 3: One-Month Automation Setup

1. Choose four themes.
2. Generate one post per theme.
3. Optimize gently with AI for SEO.
4. Schedule them across a month.
5. Step away.

Journal Prompts

1. What makes writing feel heavy for me?
2. When do I confuse effort with authenticity?
3. What emotions feel safest to express in writing?
4. Where do I overshare to feel understood?
5. How does automation change my relationship with creativity?
6. What would a "quiet success" look like for me?
7. How does distance protect my emotional health?
8. What themes do I return to again and again?
9. What does consistency feel like without pressure?
10. How can my blog exist without consuming me?

Closing Reflection

Your words deserve space without costing you energy. Automation does not erase meaning—it preserves it. By letting AI handle structure, repetition, and visibility, you free yourself to exist without constant output.

This chapter is about reclaiming writing as a refuge rather than a demand. Your blog can grow in silence. Your voice can echo without effort.

Let the posts publish themselves.

You stay intact.

Chapter 3: AI Voiceovers for Anonymous Video Creation

The Power of Being Heard Without Being Seen

Visibility has become the default currency of online influence. Faces, bodies, expressions, and personal spaces are constantly placed on display, often without regard for the emotional cost of that exposure. For emo creators, this expectation can feel invasive. There is a deep difference between being *heard* and being *seen*, and AI voiceovers allow you to choose the former without being forced into the latter.

Voice has always been intimate. It carries tone, emotion, restraint, and distance all at once. Unlike video presence, it does not demand eye contact or visual vulnerability. AI-generated voiceovers allow your ideas, moods, and messages to reach others without placing your physical identity on display.

This anonymity is not deception. It is design. You are not hiding because you are ashamed—you are choosing a medium that aligns with your emotional safety. Many emo creators communicate more honestly when the body is removed from the equation.

AI voiceovers allow you to maintain mystery while still forming connection. Listeners focus on the words, the pacing, the atmosphere. The absence of a visible narrator creates space for projection, resonance, and interpretation.

In this way, anonymity becomes a strength. Your content becomes timeless, detached from appearance, age, or performance. The message remains. You remain protected.

Why AI Voiceovers Reduce Anxiety and Burnout

Traditional video creation demands preparation, presence, and emotional regulation all at once. Lighting, appearance, facial expression, and vocal delivery stack pressure on top of pressure. For creators prone to anxiety, this can make content creation feel impossible.

AI voiceovers remove the need for emotional readiness. You do not have to feel "on" to create. You do not need to rehearse, record multiple takes, or listen to your own voice repeatedly. The emotional friction disappears.

This reduction in friction changes everything. Creation becomes logistical rather than personal. You write or prompt text, select tone and pacing, and let the system handle delivery. Your nervous system is no longer part of the production pipeline.

Burnout often comes from repetition under exposure. AI voiceovers allow repetition without self-drain. You can publish consistently without emotionally reliving the same thoughts or feelings.

For emo creators, this is not avoidance—it is sustainability. You are choosing a method that allows you to continue creating without sacrificing emotional stability.

Matching AI Voice Tone to Emo Aesthetic

One of the most common fears about AI voiceovers is that they will sound artificial, hollow, or disconnected. In reality, tone selection and pacing are what determine emotional resonance—not whether the voice is human or synthetic.

Emo aesthetics thrive on restraint. Slow cadence. Soft intensity. Controlled emotion. AI voice tools allow you to choose voices that reflect these qualities, rather than exaggerated or overly enthusiastic tones.

You can experiment with different deliveries: low and steady, distant and reflective, slightly melancholic, or calm and neutral. Each choice creates a different emotional texture without requiring you to embody it personally.

The key is consistency. Once you find a voice that matches your emotional range, it becomes part of your brand's atmosphere. Listeners come to recognize the feeling rather than the person.

This allows you to remain emotionally authentic without emotional exposure. The voice becomes a vessel, not a mirror.

Pairing AI Voiceovers with Visuals Without Oversharing

Anonymous video creation works best when voiceovers are paired with visuals that reinforce mood without revealing identity. This might include text overlays, abstract imagery, slow-moving footage, static scenes, shadows, or symbolic visuals.

AI can assist here as well—suggesting visual concepts that align with the tone of your script. You are not required to show your home, your body, or your environment. The visuals exist to support the voice, not compete with it.

This approach shifts focus from personality to presence. The audience engages with atmosphere rather than appearance. The content feels intentional rather than performative.

Visual anonymity also allows for reuse. The same style of video can be replicated across platforms without requiring new emotional input. The system becomes modular.

You are not building a personal brand in the traditional sense. You are building a *signal*—one that feels coherent, quiet, and emotionally contained.

Scaling Anonymous Content Across Platforms

AI voiceovers make cross-platform publishing far easier. The same script can be adapted into different formats without additional emotional effort. A single piece of writing can become a TikTok voiceover, an Instagram reel, a YouTube short, or part of a longer video.

This scalability is crucial for creators who want reach without constant output. You are not starting from scratch each time. You are redistributing energy efficiently.

AI can help adjust pacing, length, and structure depending on the platform. Shorter cuts for fast scroll environments. Longer, slower versions for reflective platforms.

The emotional labor remains constant while the reach expands. This prevents the feeling of being "spread thin" across platforms.

Growth no longer requires more of you. It requires better systems.

Building a Voice-Based Creative System That Protects You

The ultimate goal of AI voiceovers is not novelty—it is protection. A sustainable system allows you to create, publish, and rest without emotional whiplash.

In this system, writing becomes the only personal input. Everything else—delivery, pacing, repetition—is automated. You decide when to write and when to step away.

Over time, this builds trust with yourself. You know that your presence online does not depend on your emotional availability. The system holds when you cannot.

This is how long-term creators survive. Not by pushing harder, but by designing environments that do not demand constant exposure.

Your voice can exist without your body.
Your message can travel without draining you.
Your creativity can endure.

Exercises

Exercise 1: Script-to-Voice Conversion

1. Write a short paragraph expressing a mood or thought.
2. Remove any identifying personal details.
3. Input the text into an AI voice tool.
4. Test different tones and pacing.
5. Save the version that feels safest and most resonant.

Exercise 2: Visual Pairing Without Identity

1. Choose one voiceover script.
2. List five non-personal visual ideas that match the tone.
3. Select one and create a simple video.
4. Publish anonymously.
5. Observe how it feels emotionally.

Exercise 3: One-Week Anonymous Content Batch

1. Write three short scripts.
2. Generate AI voiceovers for each.
3. Pair with minimal visuals.
4. Schedule across platforms.
5. Step back completely.

Journal Prompts

1. What parts of visibility feel unsafe to me?
2. How does anonymity change my creative confidence?
3. What emotions feel easier to express through voice than image?
4. Where do I feel pressure to show my face unnecessarily?
5. How does removing my body from content affect my anxiety?
6. What tone feels most like "me" without exposure?
7. How does repetition feel when I'm not performing?
8. What boundaries does anonymous creation protect?
9. How does my content change when it's less personal but still honest?
10. What would long-term sustainability look like for me?

Closing Reflection

You do not owe your image to be heard. Your ideas are not less real because they arrive without a face. AI voiceovers offer a way to exist creatively without sacrificing safety, privacy, or emotional stability.

This chapter is about reclaiming control—over how you are perceived, how much you reveal, and how often you are required to show up. When the voice becomes the medium, the pressure dissolves.

Let the sound carry the meaning.

You remain unseen—and unbroken.

Chapter 4: AI Scheduling & Auto-Posting to Stay Active Without Being Online

The Illusion That You Must Always Be Present

Social media quietly teaches a dangerous belief: that visibility requires constant presence. Notifications, real-time trends, and engagement metrics reinforce the idea that if you are not actively online, you are falling behind. For emo creators—especially those sensitive to overstimulation—this belief can create chronic anxiety and a feeling of never being allowed to rest.

In reality, platforms reward consistency more than presence. Algorithms do not care whether you are emotionally available; they care whether content appears regularly. AI scheduling dismantles the myth that you must be online to remain relevant.

By separating activity from availability, you reclaim control over your time and nervous system. Your content can publish itself while you are offline, resting, or emotionally unavailable. The machine handles the timing; you handle your life.

This separation is not neglect. It is design. You are building a system that respects your limits rather than punishing them.

When presence becomes automated, absence becomes safe.

How AI Scheduling Reduces Anxiety and Burnout

Anxiety thrives on unpredictability. When posting is reactive—deciding what to share, when to share, and how it will be received—it keeps your nervous system in a constant state of alert. Scheduling replaces chaos with certainty.

When content is planned in advance, you are no longer negotiating with yourself every day. The decision-making fatigue disappears. You are not asking, "Should I post today?" The answer has already been decided by your system.

AI scheduling tools can analyze optimal posting windows without requiring you to monitor trends constantly. This removes the pressure to be awake, alert, and responsive at all times.

Burnout often comes from the emotional cost of showing up repeatedly. Automation allows you to show up without *being* there. The emotional toll drops dramatically.

Over time, your relationship with content creation shifts from reactive to intentional. Anxiety loses its grip.

Designing a Posting Rhythm That Respects Your Energy

Not all consistency is healthy. Posting daily is not inherently better than posting weekly. The goal is not maximum output—it is sustainable rhythm.

AI allows you to design a posting schedule that aligns with your energy patterns rather than fighting them. You choose frequency based on what feels safe, not what feels demanded.

For emo creators, slower rhythms often feel more authentic. Fewer posts, released intentionally, create a sense of weight and presence rather than noise. AI helps maintain that rhythm without requiring constant input.

You can schedule content during moments of clarity or calm and let it deploy later. This ensures your content reflects your grounded self rather than your overwhelmed self.

Rhythm replaces pressure. Structure replaces anxiety.

Auto-Posting Across Platforms Without Emotional Fragmentation

Managing multiple platforms often fractures emotional energy. Each platform feels like a separate demand, requiring different tones, formats, and timing. AI reduces this fragmentation by centralizing control.

With auto-posting, a single piece of content can be adapted and scheduled across Instagram, TikTok, YouTube, and blogs without additional emotional labor. You are not reinventing yourself for each platform.

AI can adjust captions, lengths, and formats automatically while preserving your core message. This ensures coherence without dilution.

The emotional benefit is significant. You feel whole rather than scattered. Your identity remains intact across platforms.

You are not multitasking emotionally. You are distributing intentionally.

Staying Active Without Being Pulled Back In

One of the hidden dangers of scheduling is the temptation to check in constantly. Metrics, comments, and notifications can pull you back into emotional engagement even when posting is automated.

AI tools can help manage this by batching engagement or delaying notifications. You choose when to interact rather than being summoned by the platform.

This creates a protective buffer. You remain active without being reactive. You are present on your terms.

For emo creators, this boundary is essential. Emotional energy is finite. Automation ensures it is spent where it matters most.

Activity no longer equals availability.

Building a Long-Term Auto-Posting System That Holds You

The true power of scheduling lies in its ability to carry your presence during periods of withdrawal, illness, burnout, or creative silence. A strong system does not collapse when you step away.

AI-driven scheduling creates continuity. Your audience experiences steadiness even when you are offline. This reduces guilt, fear of disappearance, and pressure to explain absence.

Over time, this builds trust—with your audience and with yourself. You learn that stepping away does not erase you.

The system becomes a container. It holds your work, your rhythm, and your boundaries.

You are allowed to rest. The machine will not forget you.

Exercises

Exercise 1: Energy-Aligned Schedule Mapping

1. Track your energy levels over a week.
2. Identify one or two calm windows.
3. Use AI to generate content during those windows.
4. Schedule posts outside your low-energy times.
5. Commit to not adjusting once scheduled.

Exercise 2: One-Week Auto-Posting Trial

1. Choose three pieces of content.
2. Schedule them across platforms.
3. Turn off notifications.
4. Stay offline during posting times.
5. Reflect on how it feels.

Exercise 3: Platform Consolidation Setup

1. List all platforms you use.
2. Decide which ones matter most.
3. Use AI to adapt one post for all platforms.
4. Schedule simultaneously.
5. Remove pressure to engage everywhere.

Journal Prompts

1. Where do I equate presence with worth?
2. How does constant availability affect my anxiety?
3. What posting rhythm feels safest for me?
4. Where do I feel guilt about stepping away?
5. How does automation change my sense of control?
6. What would rest look like without disappearance?
7. How do metrics influence my emotions?
8. Where can I set firmer engagement boundaries?
9. What does sustainable visibility mean to me?
10. How can systems protect my nervous system?

Closing Reflection

You were never meant to live inside the feed. Your creativity does not require constant attendance to exist. AI scheduling allows your work to move forward without dragging you along with it.

This chapter is about reclaiming time, emotional safety, and autonomy. When activity no longer demands presence, rest becomes possible without fear.

Let the posts go out on their own.

You stay offline—and whole.

Chapter 5: How to Use AI to Go Viral in the Emo & Goth Niche

Redefining "Viral" for Emo & Goth Creators

Viral success is often portrayed as loud, chaotic, and hyper-visible—everything emo and goth culture historically resists. But virality does not require brightness or noise. In these subcultures, what spreads is **recognition**. A feeling that lands. A line that aches. An image that feels like a secret finally spoken aloud.

For emo and goth creators, virality is not about pleasing everyone. It is about resonating deeply with a specific emotional frequency. AI becomes powerful here not because it manufactures trends, but because it helps you identify patterns of resonance without forcing you to abandon your identity.

When a post goes viral in this niche, it is usually quiet at first. It spreads through saves, shares, duets, stitches, reposts, and late-night reblogs. AI can analyze these patterns—what gets saved versus liked, what is shared privately rather than publicly—so you understand *why* something spreads without guessing.

This reframes virality as **emotional alignment**, not performance. You are not chasing attention; you are tuning a signal. AI helps you refine that signal without diluting it.

Going viral, then, becomes repeatable—not because you copy yourself, but because you understand the emotional mechanics beneath the spread.

Using AI to Identify Emotional Triggers That Spread

Every viral emo or goth post activates one or more emotional triggers: nostalgia, alienation, longing, quiet rage, romantic despair, aesthetic isolation, or defiant softness. These triggers are not trends—they are constants. AI helps you surface them intentionally.

By analyzing comments, captions, and high-performing content within the niche, AI can reveal which emotions are being named, implied, or echoed most often. This does not mean you must imitate others. It means you can recognize what your audience already feels but struggles to articulate.

AI allows you to test phrasing without self-exposure. You can ask it to generate multiple versions of a caption or script, each leaning into a different emotional trigger, and then choose the one that feels truest. This removes the anxiety of "getting it wrong" publicly.

Importantly, AI also helps you avoid emotional overreach. Some triggers spread fast but burn out quickly. Others create slower, deeper waves. You get to choose which kind of virality aligns with your boundaries.

When emotion is handled intentionally, virality becomes a side effect—not a gamble.

Crafting Viral Emo Content Without Oversharing

One of the most common mistakes in emotional niches is equating virality with confession. Oversharing may attract attention, but it often leaves creators feeling exposed, depleted, or trapped by an audience that expects continual access. AI helps you avoid this trap.

AI excels at **symbolic compression**—turning personal experiences into universal language. Instead of sharing a specific story, you share a feeling. Instead of naming a wound, you describe the atmosphere around it. This invites projection rather than voyeurism.

For example, AI can help you rewrite content to remove identifying details while keeping emotional weight intact. It can shift from "this happened to me" to "this feeling exists," preserving privacy without losing resonance.

This is especially powerful for video captions, voiceovers, and short-form text, where less specificity often increases shareability. People share what feels like *them*, not what feels like *you*.

Virality increases when the audience can inhabit the content without crossing your boundaries. AI helps maintain that line consistently.

Timing, Format, and Aesthetic Amplification with AI

Virality is not just about what you say—it's about when and how it appears. Emo and goth audiences often engage at different times and in different ways than mainstream creators. Late nights, early mornings, seasonal shifts, and emotional cycles all matter.

AI can analyze posting times, aesthetic formats, and pacing that perform best in this niche without requiring you to monitor constantly. You learn when your audience is most receptive without being perpetually online.

Format also matters. Short text-on-screen videos, slow pans over static imagery, whispered or monotone voiceovers, and minimalist captions often outperform high-energy content in these spaces. AI helps you test formats without exhausting yourself.

Aesthetic amplification means reinforcing mood consistently. AI can suggest color palettes, visual motifs, and caption structures that align with emo and goth sensibilities—dark minimalism, romantic decay, restrained intensity.

Virality becomes less about luck and more about alignment between timing, format, and feeling.

Scaling Viral Moments Without Emotional Whiplash

One viral post often leads to pressure: post more, explain more, engage more. This is where many creators burn out. AI allows you to scale momentum without increasing emotional exposure.

When a post performs well, AI can help you generate follow-ups that echo the theme without repeating the same emotional labor. You are extending a resonance, not reopening a wound.

You can also use AI to repurpose viral content across platforms—turning a caption into a voiceover, a voiceover into a blog post, a blog post into a short-form quote—without re-creating from scratch.

This creates continuity rather than escalation. Your audience experiences depth, not desperation. You stay grounded while the content spreads.

Scaling does not require intensity. It requires systems.

Making Virality Sustainable and Intentional

The final shift is internal. Virality should not become the goal—it should become a tool. AI helps you decide what kind of attention you want and what kind you are unwilling to hold.

Sustainable virality respects cycles. Some posts will spread widely. Others will remain quiet. Both are valid. AI helps normalize this by showing patterns rather than spikes.

You learn to treat viral moments as data, not validation. This protects your sense of self from metrics and external reaction.

When used intentionally, AI allows you to grow without chasing relevance. You become discoverable without becoming consumed.

Virality becomes something that passes through your work—not something that takes you over.

Exercises

Exercise 1: Emotional Trigger Mapping

1. List five emotions central to your aesthetic.
2. Ask AI to generate three content ideas per emotion.
3. Remove any ideas that feel too personal.
4. Select one to publish.
5. Observe resonance without over-engaging.

Exercise 2: One Viral Rewrite Test

1. Choose a post that performed well.
2. Ask AI to rewrite it three ways using different emotional tones.
3. Publish one version.
4. Save the others for later.
5. Note which version feels safest and strongest.

Exercise 3: Viral Momentum Buffer

1. Identify one piece of content gaining traction.
2. Use AI to create two adjacent follow-ups.
3. Schedule them in advance.
4. Turn off notifications.
5. Let momentum unfold without interference.

Journal Prompts

1. What does "viral" mean to me emotionally?
2. Which emotions feel most shareable without harm?
3. Where do I confuse attention with connection?
4. How does oversharing affect my sense of safety?
5. What kind of audience do I actually want?
6. How do metrics influence my self-worth?
7. What boundaries protect me during growth?
8. How does AI change my relationship with risk?
9. What would slow virality feel like?
10. How can attention serve me rather than consume me?

Closing Reflection

Virality does not have to cost you your privacy, your stability, or your identity. In the emo and goth niche, what spreads is not spectacle—it is truth wrapped in restraint.

AI allows you to approach virality with intention instead of fear. You can study resonance without sacrificing yourself to it. You can grow without becoming visible in ways that feel unsafe.

Let the signal travel.

You remain grounded, guarded, and intact.

Appendix A: AI Social Media Growth Tools

This appendix is designed as a **practical reference**, not a sales pitch. The tools described here are presented by **function and role**, not as endorsements or guarantees. You do not need every tool listed. You only need the ones that reduce emotional labor, protect your energy, and support sustainable growth.

AI tools should work **for you**, not pull you deeper into the attention economy.

1. AI Writing & Caption Generation Tools

These tools assist with **text-based creation**: captions, descriptions, scripts, hooks, blog posts, comments, and replies. Their primary value is reducing the cognitive and emotional effort required to "find the words."

What They Do Well

- Generate multiple caption variations from a single mood or theme
- Rewrite text to sound more poetic, restrained, or emotionally neutral
- Adapt tone for different platforms without changing meaning
- Help avoid oversharing by abstracting personal language
- Speed up ideation without forcing emotional immersion

Best Use for Emo & Goth Creators

- Creating ambiguous, atmospheric captions
- Translating emotions into symbolic language
- Maintaining consistent voice across platforms
- Writing without reliving emotional experiences

Use With Care

- Always review for emotional boundaries
- Remove anything that feels too revealing
- Avoid letting the tool define your identity

These tools are most effective when used as **co-writers**, not replacements.

2. AI Voiceover & Text-to-Speech Tools

Voiceover tools convert written scripts into spoken audio, allowing anonymous video creation and emotional distance from performance.

What They Do Well

- Convert scripts into calm, neutral, or melancholic voices
- Offer multiple voice styles and pacing options
- Remove the need to record or edit your own voice
- Create consistent delivery across multiple videos
- Reduce anxiety around speaking or appearance

Best Use for Emo & Goth Creators

- Anonymous TikTok, Reels, and Shorts
- Atmospheric YouTube narration
- Whispered, monotone, or reflective delivery
- Voice-based storytelling without exposure

Use With Care

- Choose voices that feel restrained, not theatrical
- Keep pacing slow and intentional
- Avoid overproduction that breaks intimacy

Voiceover tools are ideal when you want **presence without visibility**.

3. AI Video Editing & Visual Generation Tools

These tools support the **visual side** of content creation without requiring filming, appearance, or physical staging.

What They Do Well

- Generate background visuals, abstract imagery, or symbolic scenes
- Assist with text-on-screen animations
- Automate transitions, pacing, and formatting
- Create repeatable visual templates
- Reduce time spent editing

Best Use for Emo & Goth Creators

- Minimalist, moody visuals
- Static or slow-moving imagery
- Shadow, grain, blur, and low-contrast aesthetics
- Reusable formats that don't demand creativity every time

Use With Care

- Avoid visuals that feel too polished or commercial
- Keep aesthetic consistent across posts
- Let the mood lead, not the effects

These tools should support atmosphere, not distract from it.

4. AI Scheduling & Auto-Posting Tools

Scheduling tools automate **when and where** your content appears, allowing you to remain offline while staying active.

What They Do Well

- Schedule posts across multiple platforms
- Optimize posting times without manual tracking
- Maintain consistency during rest or burnout
- Reduce decision fatigue
- Separate creation from publication

Best Use for Emo & Goth Creators

- Low-frequency, intentional posting rhythms
- Batch scheduling during calm periods
- Staying present without constant engagement
- Protecting emotional boundaries

Use With Care

- Don't over-schedule to the point of pressure
- Turn off unnecessary notifications
- Avoid checking metrics compulsively

Scheduling tools are about **freedom**, not productivity.

5. AI Analytics & Pattern Recognition Tools

These tools analyze engagement data to help you understand what resonates—without relying on emotional reaction.

What They Do Well

- Identify which posts are saved, shared, or revisited
- Highlight emotional themes that resonate most
- Track slow-burn content performance
- Reduce guesswork around virality
- Turn growth into information, not validation

Best Use for Emo & Goth Creators

- Understanding resonance without obsession
- Identifying safe emotional triggers
- Refining tone and pacing
- Avoiding burnout from guessing

Use With Care

- Do not tie metrics to self-worth
- Avoid checking daily
- Use data to guide systems, not identity

Analytics should inform—not define—you.

6. AI Repurposing & Content Expansion Tools

These tools help turn one piece of content into many formats without additional emotional labor.

What They Do Well

- Convert captions into scripts
- Turn videos into blog posts
- Extract quotes from long content
- Adapt tone for different platforms
- Extend viral moments safely

Best Use for Emo & Goth Creators

- Scaling reach without oversharing
- Maintaining consistency without repetition
- Reusing emotional energy efficiently
- Building archives instead of constant output

Use With Care

- Avoid emotional dilution
- Maintain intentional pacing
- Stop when it feels like "too much"

Repurposing is about **containment**, not saturation.

7. How to Choose the Right Tools for You

You do not need a large stack. In fact, fewer tools often mean less anxiety.

Ask yourself:

- Does this tool reduce emotional labor?
- Does it protect my privacy and boundaries?
- Does it allow me to rest without disappearing?
- Does it support my aesthetic rather than override it?

If the answer is no, you don't need it.

The best AI tools disappear into your workflow. They do their job quietly, without demanding attention or performance.

Final Note on Tools and Autonomy

AI tools are not shortcuts to success. They are **buffers**—between you and constant visibility, between creativity and exhaustion, between expression and exposure.

Used intentionally, they allow you to:

- Create without anxiety
- Grow without burnout
- Be present without being consumed

The tools exist to serve your nervous system, your boundaries, and your longevity.

Choose the ones that let you stay mysterious.

Discard the rest.

<u>Message from the Author:</u>

I hope you enjoyed this book, I love astrology and knew there was not a book such as this out on the shelf. I love metaphysical items as well. Please check out my other books:

-Life of Government Benefits

-My life of Hell

-My life with Hydrocephalus

-Red Sky

-World Domination:Woman's rule

-World Domination:Woman's Rule 2: The War

-Life and Banishment of Apophis: book 1

-The Kidney Friendly Diet

-The Ultimate Hemp Cookbook

-Creating a Dispensary(legally)

-Cleanliness throughout life: the importance of showering from childhood to adulthood.

-Strong Roots: The Risks of Overcoddling children

-Hemp Horoscopes: Cosmic Insights and Earthly Healing

- Celestial Hemp Navigating the Zodiac: Through the Green Cosmos

-Astrological Hemp: Aligning The Stars with Earth's Ancient Herb

-The Astrological Guide to Hemp: Stars, Signs, and Sacred Leaves

-Green Growth: Innovative Marketing Strategies for your Hemp Products and Dispensary

-Cosmic Cannabis

-Astrological Munchies

-Henry The Hemp

-Zodiacal Roots: The Astrological Soul Of Hemp

- **Green Constellations: Intersection of Hemp and Zodiac**

-Hemp in The Houses: An astrological Adventure Through The Cannabis Galaxy

-Galactic Ganja Guide
Heavenly Hemp
Zodiac Leaves
Doctor Who Astrology
Cannastrology
Stellar Satvias and Cosmic Indicas
Celestial Cannabis: A Zodiac Journey
AstroHerbology: The Sky and The Soil: Volume 1
AstroHerbology:Celestial Cannabis:Volume 2
Cosmic Cannabis Cultivation
The Starry Guide to Herbal Harmony: Volume 1
The Starry Guide to Herbal Harmony: Cannabis Universe: Volume 2
Yugioh Astrology: Astrological Guide to Deck, Duels and more
Nightmare Mansion: Echoes of The Abyss
Nightmare Mansion 2: Legacy of Shadows
Nightmare Mansion 3: Shadows of the Forgotten
Nightmare Mansion 4: Echoes of the Damned
The Life and Banishment of Apophis: Book 2
Nightmare Mansion: Halls of Despair
Healing with Herb: Cannabis and Hydrocephalus
Planetary Pot: Aligning with Astrological Herbs: Volume 1
Fast Track to Freedom: 30 Days to Financial Independence Using AI, Assets, and Agile Hustles
Cosmic Hemp Pathways
How to Become Financially Free in 30 Days: 10,000 Paths to Prosperity
Zodiacal Herbage: Astrological Insights: Volume 1
Nightmare Mansion: Whispers in the Walls
The Daleks Invade Atlantis
Henry the hemp and Hydrocephalus

10X The Kidney Friendly Diet

Cannabis Universe: Adult coloring book

Hemp Astrology: The Healing Power of the Stars

Zodiacal Herbage: Astrological Insights: Cannabis Universe: Volume 2

Planetary Pot: Aligning with Astrological Herbs: Cannabis Universes: Volume 2

Doctor Who: Convergence Protocol – The Replicator War

Nightmare Mansion: Curse of the Blood Moon

The Celestial Stoner: A Guide to the Zodiac

Cosmic Pleasures: Sex Toy Astrology for Every Sign

Hydrocephalus Astrology: Navigating the Stars and Healing Waters

Lapis and the Mischievous Chocolate Bar

Celestial Positions: Sexual Astrology for Every Sign

Apophis's Shadow Work Journal: **:** A Journey of Self-Discovery and Healing

Kinky Cosmos: Sexual Kink Astrology for Every Sign

Digital Cosmos: The Astrological Digimon Compendium

Stellar Seeds: The Cosmic Guide to Growing with Astrology

Apophis's Daily Gratitude Journal

Cat Astrology: Feline Mysteries of the Cosmos

The Cosmic Kama Sutra: An Astrological Guide to Sexual Positions

Unleash Your Potential: A Guided Journal Powered by AI Insights

Whispers of the Enchanted Grove

Cosmic Pleasures: An Astrological Guide to Sexual Kinks

369, 12 Manifestation Journal

Whisper of the nocturne journal(blank journal for writing or drawing)

The Boogey Book

Locked In Reflection: A Chastity Journey Through Locktober

Generating Wealth Quickly:How to Generate $100,000 in 24 Hours

Star Magic: Harness the Power of the Universe

The Flatulence Chronicles: A Fart Journal for Self-Discovery

The Doctor and The Death Moth

Seize the Day: A Personal Seizure Tracking Journal

The Ultimate Boogeyman Safari: A Journey into the Boogie World and Beyond

Whispers of Samhain: 1,000 Spells of Love, Luck, and Lunar Magic: Samhain Spell Book

Apophis's guides:Witch's Spellbook Crafting Guide for Halloween

Frost & Flame: The Enchanted Yule Grimoire of 1000 Winter Spells

The Ultimate Boogey Goo Guide & Spooky Activities for Halloween Fun

Harmony of the Scales: A Libra's Spellcraft for Balance and Beauty

The Enchanted Advent: 36 Days of Christmas Wonders

Nightmare Mansion: The Labyrinth of Screams

Harvest of Enchantment: 1,000 Spells of Gratitude, Love, and Fortune for Thanksgiving

The Boogey Chronicles: A Journal of Nightly Encounters and Shadowy Secrets

The 12 Days of Financial Freedom: A Step-by-Step Christmas Countdown to Transform Your Finances

Sigil of the Eternal Spiral Blank Journal

A Christmas Feast: Timeless Recipes for Every Meal

Holiday Stress-Free Solutions: A Survival Guide to Thriving During the Festive Season

Yu-Gi-Oh! Holiday Gifting Mastery: The Ultimate Guide for Fans and Newcomers Alike

Holiday Harmony: A Hydrocephalus Survival Guide for the Festive Season

Celestial Craft: The Witch's Almanac for 2025 – A Cosmic Guide to Manifestations, Moons, and Mystical Events

Doctor Who: The Toymaker's Winter Wonderland

Tulsa King Unveiled: A Thrilling Guide to Stallone's Mafia Masterpiece

Pendulum Craft: A Complete Guide to Crafting and Using Personalized Divination Tools

Nightmare Mansion: Santa's Eternal Eve

Starlight Noel: A Cosmic Journey through Christmas Mysteries

The Dark Architect: Unlocking the Blueprint of Existence

Surviving the Embrace: The Ultimate Guide to Encounters with The Hugging Molly

The Enchanted Codex: Secrets of the Craft for Witches, Wiccans, and Pagans

Harvest of Gratitude: A Complete Thanksgiving Guide

Yuletide Essentials: A Complete Guide to an Authentic and Magical Christmas

Celestial Smokes: A Cosmic Guide to Cigars and Astrology

Living in Balance: A Comprehensive Survival Guide to Thriving with Diabetes Insipidus

Cosmic Symbiosis: The Venom Zodiac Chronicles

The Cursed Paw of Ambition

Cosmic Symbiosis: The Astrological Venom Journal

Celestial Wonders Unfold: A Stargazer's Guide to the Cosmos (2024-2029)

The Ultimate Black Friday Prepper's Guide: Mastering Shopping Strategies and Savings

Cosmic Sales: The Astrological Guide to Black Friday Shopping

Legends of the Corn Mother and Other Harvest Myths

Whispers of the Harvest: The Corn Mother's Journal

The Evergreen Spellbook

The Doctor Meets the Boogeyman

The White Witch of Rose Hall's SpellBook

The Gingerbread Golem's Shadow: A Study in Sweet Darkness

The Gingerbread Golem Codex: An Academic Exploration of Sweet Myths

The Gingerbread Golem Grimoire: Sweet Magicks and Spells for the Festive Witch

The Curse of the Gingerbread Golem

10-minute Christmas Crafts for kids

Christmas Crisis Solutions: The Ultimate Last-Minute Survival Guide

Gingerbread Golem Recipes: Holiday Treats with a Magical Twist

The Infinite Key: Unlocking Mystical Secrets of the Ages

Enchanted Yule: A Wiccan and Pagan Guide to a Magical and Memorable Season

Dinosaurs of Power: Unlocking Ancient Magick

Astro-Dinos: The Cosmic Guide to Prehistoric Wisdom

Gallifrey's Yule Logs: A Festive Doctor Who Cookbook

The Dino Grimoire: Secrets of Prehistoric Magick

The Gift They Never Knew They Needed

The Gingerbread Golem's Culinary Alchemy: Enchanting Recipes for a Sweetly Dark Feast

A Time Lord Christmas: Holiday Adventures with the Doctor

Krampusproofing Your Home: Defensive Strategies for Yule

Silent Frights: A Collection of Christmas Creepypastas to Chill Your Bones

Santa Raptor's Jolly Carnage: A Dino-Claus Christmas Tale

Prehistoric Palettes: A Dino Wicca Coloring Journey

The Christmas Wishkeeper Chronicles

The Starlight Sleigh: A Holiday Journey

Elf Secrets: The True Magic of the North Pole

Candy Cane Conjurations
Cooking with Kids: Recipes Under 20 Minutes
Doctor Who: The TARDIS Confiscation
The Anxiety First Aid Kit: Quick Tools to Calm Your Mind
Frosty Whispers: A Winter's Tale
The Infinite Key: Unlocking the Secrets to Prosperity, Resilience, and Purpose
The Grasping Void: Why You'll Regret This Purchase
Astrology for Busy Bees: Star Signs Simplified
The Instant Focus Formula: Cut Through the Noise
The Secret Language of Colors: Unlocking the Emotional Codes
Sacred Fossil Chronicles: Blank Journal
The Christmas Cottage Miracle
Feeding Frenzy: Graboid-Inspired Recipes
Manifest in Minutes: The Quick Law of Attraction Guide
The Symbiote Chronicles: Doctor Who's Venomous Journey
Think Tiny, Grow Big: The Minimalist Mindset
The Energy Key: Unlocking Limitless Motivation
New Year, New Magic: Manifesting Your Best Year Yet
Unstoppable You: Mastering Confidence in Minutes
Infinite Energy: The Secret to Never Feeling Drained
Lightning Focus: Mastering the Art of Productivity in a Distracted World
Saturnalia Manifestation Magick: A Guide to Unlocking Abundance During the Solstice
Graboids and Garland: The Ultimate Tremors-Themed Christmas Guide
12 Nights of Holiday Magic
The Power of Pause: 60-Second Mindfulness Practices
The Quick Reset: How to Reclaim Your Life After Burnout
The Shadow Eater: A Tale of Despair and Survival
The Micro-Mastery Method: Transform Your Skills in Just Minutes a Day

Reclaiming Time: How to Live More by Doing Less
Chronovore: The Eternal Nexus
The Mind Reset: Unlocking Your Inner Peace in a Chaotic World
Confidence Code: Building Unshakable Self-Belief
Baby the Vampire Terrier
Baby the Vampire Terrier's Christmas Adventure
Celestial Streams: The Content Creator's Astrology Manual
The Wealth Whisperer: Unlocking Abundance with Everyday Actions
The Energy Equation: Maximize Your Output Without Burning Out
The Happiness Algorithm: Science-Backed Steps to Joyful Living
Stress-Free Success: Achieving Goals Without Anxiety
Mindful Wealth: The New Blueprint for Financial Freedom
The Festive Flavors of New Year: A Culinary Celebration
The Master's Gambit: Keys of Eternal Power
Shadowed Secrets: Groundhog Day Mysteries
Beneath the Burrow: Lessons from the Groundhog
Spring's Whispers: The Groundhog's Prediction
The Limitless Mindset: Unlock Your Untapped Potential
The Focus Funnel: How to Cut Through Chaos and Get Results
Bold Moves: Building Courage to Live on Your Terms
The Daily Shift: Simple Practices for Lasting Transformation
The Quarter-Life Reset: Thriving in Your 20s and 30s
The Art of Shadowplay: Building Your Own Personal Myth
The Eternal Loop: Finding Purpose in Repetition
Burrowing Wisdom: Life Lessons from the Groundhog
Shadow Work: A Groundhog Day Perspective
Love in Bloom: 5-Minute Romantic Gestures
The Shadowspell Codex: Secrets of Forbidden Magick
The Burnout Cure: Finding Balance in a Busy World
The Groundhog Prophecy: Unlocking Seasonal Secrets
Nog Tales: The Spirited History of Eggnog

Six More Weeks: Embracing Seasonal Transitions
The Lumivian Chronicles: Fragments of the Fifth Dimension
Money on Your Mind: A Beginner's Guide to Wealth
The Focus Fix: Breaking Through Distraction
January's Spirit Keepers: Mystical Protectors of the Cold
Creativity Unchained: Unlocking Your Wildest Ideas in 2025
Manifestation Mastery: 365 Days to Rewrite Your Reality
The Groundhog's Mirror: Reflecting on Change
The Weeping Angels' Christmas Curse
Burrowed in Time: A Groundhog Day Journey
Heartbeats: Poems to Share with Your Valentine
Dino Wicca: The Sacred Grimoire of Prehistoric Magick
Courage of the Pride: Finding Your Inner Roar
The Lion's Leap: Bold Moves for Big Results
Healthy Hustle: Achieving Without Overworking
Practical Manifesting: Turning Dreams into Reality in 2025
Jurassic Pharaohs: Unlocking the Magick of Ancient Egypt and Dino Wicca
The Happiness Equation: Small Changes for Big Joy
The Confidence Compass: Finding Your Inner Strength
Whispers in the Hollow: Tales of the Forgotten Beasts
Echoes from the Hollow: The Return of Forgotten Beasts
The Hollow Ascendant: The Rise of the Forgotten Beasts
The Relationship Reset: Building Better Connections
Mastering the Morning: How to Win the Day Before 8 AM
The Shadow's Dance: Groundhog Day Symbolism
Cupid's Kitchen: Quick Valentine's Day Recipes
Valentine's Day on a Budget: Love Without Breaking the Bank
Astrocraft: Aligning the Stars in the World of Minecraft
Forecasting Life: Groundhog Day Reflections
Bleeding Hearts: Twisted Tales of Valentine's Terror
Herbal Smoke Revolution: The Ultimate Guide to Nature's Cigarette Alternative

Winter's Wrath: The Complete Survival Blueprint for Extreme Freezes.

The Groundhog's Shadow: A Tale of Seasons

Burrowed Insights: Wisdom from the Groundhog

Sensual Strings: The Art of Erotic Bondage

Whispered Flames: Unlocking the Power of Fire Play

Forgotten Shadows: A Guide to Cryptids Lost to Time

Six Weeks of Secrets: Groundhog Day's Hidden Messages

Shadows and Cycles: Groundhog Day Reflections

The Art of Love Letters: Crafting the Perfect Message

Romantic Getaways at Home: Turning Your Space into Paradise

Purrfect Brews: A Cat Lover's Guide to Coffee and Companionship

The Groundhog's Wisdom: Timeless Lessons for Modern Life

The Shadow Oracle: Groundhog Day as a Predictor

Emerging from the Burrow: A Journey of Renewal

The Language of Love: Learning Your Partner's Love Style

Authorpreneur: The Ultimate Blueprint for Writing, Publishing, and Thriving as an Author

Weathering the Seasons: Groundhog Day Perspectives

Valentine's Day Magic: A Guide to Romantic Rituals

The Shadow Chronicles: Stories of Groundhog Day

Love and Laughter: Fun Games for Valentine's Day

AstroRealty: Unlocking the Stars for Property Success

The Groundhog's Path: A Guide to Seasonal Balance

Groundhog Day Diaries: Reflections in the Shadow

The Groundhog's Light: Illuminating the Path Ahead

Valentine's Traditions from Around the World

AI Wealth Revolution: Unlocking the Trillionaire Mindset

Love Rekindled: Reigniting Passion in Relationships

Single and Thriving: Self-Love on Valentine's Day

Emerald Legends: Mystical Tales of Ireland

Green Alchemy: Harnessing Nature's Magic
The Hearts of Horror: A Valentine's Day Nightmare
The Leprechaun's Guide to Wealth and Wisdom
Dancing with the Sidhe: Celebrating the Otherworld
Shamrocks and Shadows: Mysteries of the Green Isle
Emerald Energy: Harnessing Luck and Growth
The Gingerbread Golem's Valentine: A Sweetheart's Guide to Love and Enchantment
The Celtic Knot: Weaving Life and Destiny
Green Fire: Elemental Magic for St. Patrick's Day
Clover Chronicles: Finding Your Inner Luck
Ireland's Mystical Creatures: A Field Guide
Gingerbread Golem's Love Almanac
Prowl and Thrive: The Lion's Guide to Success
Love Alchemy: Transforming Your Life Through Heart Energy
WORLD DOMINATION: Woman's Rule 3:The New Life
The Midnight Rose: A Guide to Lunar Love Spells
The Forbidden Letters: Writing Your Own Love Prophecy
Luck and Lore: St. Patrick's Day for Modern Mystics
The Green Path: A Pagan Celebration of Renewal
The Dark Architect's Guide to Reprogramming Reality
Prankster's Paradise: A Guide to Harmless Hijinks
Manifest Your Reality: The Law of Attraction Simplified
The TARDIS Owner's Manual: Understanding the Doctor's Ship: *A complete guide to the TARDIS, its technology, secrets, and mysteries*
Starlit Romance: Astrology Secrets for Finding True Love
The Time Lord's Atlas: A Complete Guide to the Whoniverse: ***A breakdown of the locations, planets, and dimensions explored in Doctor Who***
Sweetheart Shadows: The Dark Side of Love and Attraction
February Fire: Reigniting Passion in Every Area of Life

The Self-Love Toolkit: 5 Ways to Embrace Who You Are
February Sparks: Ignite Your Dreams in 28 Days
March to Success: A 31-Day Action Blueprint
Ancient Paths: The 13 Sacred Principles of Dino Wicca
Echoes of Tomorrow: Navigating the AI Revolution
The Wellness Blueprint: Balancing Mind, Body, and Soul
Green Horizons: Sustainable Living for a Better Tomorrow
The AI Wealth Code: How to Make Millions with Automation
AI-Powered Creativity: Writing, Art, and Music for Profit
Extinction Rites: Rebirthing Your Soul Through Prehistoric Magick
Sacred Serpents tarot
Celestial Enchantment blank journal
Star Strains
Culinary Journeys: Exploring Global Flavors at Home
The Hollowvale Curse
The Hollowvale Harvest
The Egg of Transformation: Awakening Your Inner Power
Blooming Into Power: A Wiccan Guide to Spring Awakening
The Nightmare Nexus: The Third Doctor's Perilous Haunting
Digital Detox: Reclaiming Your Life in a Connected World
Ostara's Path: Walking the Spiral of Renewal
The Sacred Hare
Financial Freedom: Building Wealth in the Modern Age
Spring's Cauldron: Stirring the Waters of Change
The Hollowvale Pact
Quantum Consciousness: The Science of Reality Shifting
The Hollowvale Hunger
The Sacred Waters Within: A Witch's Guide to Hydrocephalus Magick
The Raven's Nest: Building a Life of Unshakable Stability
AI and the Human Mind: The Future of Intelligence
The Hollowvale Reckoning

Timeless Love: Building and Maintaining Lasting Relationships

The Raven's Roar: Unlocking Unstoppable Confidence

Raven Sight: Awakening Intuition and Inner Wisdom

The Butterfly Effect: Small Changes, Big Transformations

Taming the Boogeyman: How to Conquer Your Inner Fears

The Magick of Green: Awakening Earth's Energy in You

The Entrepreneurial Mindset: Secrets to Business Success

The Hollowvale End

The Shadow Luck Ritual: Reclaiming Power from Your Dark Side

Spring Magick for Beginners: A Simple Guide to Seasonal Energy Work

Doctor Who: The Hollowvale Conundrum

The March of Miracles: Unlocking Synchronicities in Spring

Unveiling the Cosmos: A Guide to Stargazing and Space Exploration

The Ultimate Guide to Surviving an Economic Collapse

The AI Gold Rush: How to Profit from the AI Revolution

Bastet's Shadow: The Hidden Power of Feline Magick

The Bastet Codex: Unlocking the Goddess's Magickal Secrets

Purring Spells: Harnessing Bastet's Healing Frequencies

Bastet's Nine Lives: Rebirth, Transformation, and Immortality Spells

Primal Currents: Hydrocephalus Magick in the Path of Dino Wicca

The Digital Gold Rush: Mastering E-Commerce and Online Sales

Future Shock: Adapting to the Next Decade of Change

The Quantum Mindset: Think Like a Billionaire

Sacred Motherhood: Awakening the Divine Feminine Within

The Mother's Spellbook: Enchantments for Love, Protection, and Prosperity

The Witch's Guide to Parenting: Raising Empowered and Intuitive Children

The Magick of Motherhood: Reclaiming Your Power Through Rituals

The Pagan Path to Self-Love: A Goddess's Guide to Worth and Confidence

Wild Woman Magick: Unleashing Your Primal Power

The Money Magnet Blueprint: Unlocking Unlimited Wealth

Biohacking 101: Unlock Your Body's Full Potential

The Wild Father: A Pagan Guide to Strength and Wisdom

The Sacred Masculine: Unlocking Your Inner Power

The Druid's Compass

The Warrior's Mindset

The Father's Fire

Odin's Path

Ancestral Bonds

The House That Whispers

The Magician's Code

The Wild Hunt

The Green Man's Path

The Altar of Success

The Shadow and the Sword

The High Priestess's Guide to Energy Healing

The Lunar Mother

The Sacred Self-Care Grimoire

The Womb Wisdom Codex

The Wheel of the Mother

The Witch's Guide to Manifestation

The Q2 Reset

The Ultimate Guide to AI-Powered Passive Income

Escape the 9-5

AI Feline Fortunes

The Tear-Stained Grimoire

Razorblade Runes
Cemetery Sirens
The Midnight Wristwatch
The Town That Forgets
AI Horror & Creepypasta
The Hollow Frequency
The Breach Echo
The Quiet Between Worlds
The Sigil of Tharan-Khul
Summon the Vault of Y'ha'ten
The Becoming Codex
The Profit of Az'ra-nar
The Drowned Logos
Echoes of the Eldritch Will
The Deep Ledger
Necronomicon of Networth
Covenant of the Wealthwyrm
The Whisperer's Manifesto
The Rites of Azh-K'luth
The Ark of the Crawling Coin
The Tithe of Shadows
Inkheart Abyss
The Timewinds of Y'ha-nthlei
The Spiral Labyrinth of Azag-Nirrh
The Gallifreyan Heresy of the Black Pharaoh
The Psalms of Nyog-Sotha
Black Rain Alchemy
The Infinite Maw
The Entropic Blueprint
The Oracle of Sh'guul
The Book of Breach
The Drowned Saint's Testament
Dreamcraft of the Sleeper God

The Silence Market
Cthonomics: The Dark Wealth Algorithm
Invocation of the Ten-Eyed King
Wealthbound to the Wyrm Below
Become the Unnameable
Codex of the Sovereign Flame
Rituals of Relentless Becoming
The Shadow Ascends
The Eyes Beneath You
The Will That Wakes Worlds
Silence Is a Weapon
The Mirror That Screams
The Whisper Between Moments
The Mind That Devours Fear
The Myth of the Finished Self
The Architect of Your Madness
The Voice You've Buried
The Discipline of Madness
Stormborn: Awakening Your Inner Tempest
The Mind That Ate Time
Unbind Your Becoming
The Pact You Owe Yourself
The Devourer's Diet
The Acid That Carves the Path
The Tower You Must Burn
The Breath Between Worlds
Speak Like the Deep
The Labyrinth Within
The Spine of the Sea God
Rejection Is a Portal
The Crown You Refused
The Scar Is the Spell
The Lightless Flame

The Habit of Becoming Horrific
ChickenJockey Chaos
The Gatekeeper Within
You Are Not Your Name
The Compass of the Mad
The Archive of Unsent Letters
What the Mirror Can't Show You
The Knife You Needed
Worship Nothing, Become Everything
The Other Voice
The Body the World Forgot
The Vein of the Void
The Black Bone Codex
The Puzzle of the Hidden Self (Millennium Puzzle)
The Eye That Sees the Lie *(Millennium Eye)*
The Ring of Return (Millennium Ring)
The Rod of Relentless Will ***(Millennium Rod)***
The Tally of the Soul (Millennium Tauk/Necklace)
The Key to the Locked Timeline (Millennium Key)
The Scale of Sacred Decisions (Millennium Scales)
Inferno Bites: The UnOfficial Minecraft Lava Cookbook
Rot in the Attic
Prana: The Hidden Force of Your Infinite Self
The Shadow Realm Within: Transforming Darkness Into Destiny
The Borderland Collapse
Claws of Protection: Bastet's Defensive Magick
Mr. Ring-a-Ding's Madness
Yugioh Astrology: Celestial Deckcraft and Duel Destiny (2026–2027 Edition)
The Seal You Signed: Unlocking the Power You Once Feared
The Puzzle of Infinite Minds: Unlocking the Mentalism Hidden Within

The Eye That Mirrors the All: Secrets of Inner Reflection
Doctor Who: The Toymaker's Broadcast
The Rod of Eternal Flow: Commanding the Currents of Vibration
Golden Eyes of Bastet: Enhancing Psychic Vision
The Key of Dual Forces: Balance Within the Polarity
The Scales of Living Rhythm: Timing the Dance of Life
The Necklace of Hidden Cause: Weaving the Webs of Fate
The Ring of Secret Masters: Rising Through the All Within All
Daggers of the Dying Deep
Bastet's Wealth and Fortune Magick: Prosperity Rituals of the Goddess
The Tide that Speaks
The Scrolls of Petosiris: 13 Rituals from the Feathered Eye
Petosiris and the Living Plague of Osirion
Feline Fire: Bastet's Passion and Love Magick
The Star Altar of Petosiris
Bastet's Whiskers: Supernatural Sensory Magick
The Bastet Grimoire
Feeding the Shadows
The Mouthless Prayer
The Spiral Wound
Becoming the Ibis: Lessons from Petosiris's Mind
The Crimson Coven: Cola Magick for Sweet Dominion
Sacred Cat's Paw
The Soda Zodiac: A Flavor for Every Sign
Covenant of the Crawling Flame
The Ink of Ish'Zur
Frothroot: The Thirst That Ate the World
The Golden Glyphs of Prosperity
The Etherbind Codex
Echoes of the Resistance: Reclaiming the You That Survived

Harnessed Minds: Breaking Free from Mental Control
The Eyes in the Smoke
Rootwake: The Carbon Covenant
Skitter Logic: Unlearning the Fear That Built You
Doctor Who: The World That Froths
Rootwake: The Fizz That Rewrites Flesh
Rootwake: Frothfather of the World
The Holly Pact: Blood Beneath the Mistletoe
The 2nd Mass Principle: Building Unbreakable Tribes
Web of Wits: A Survival Guide to Encounters with Anasi the Spider (Aunt Nancy)
The Hexbreaking Handbook: Effective Spells to Remove Curses
Pop Alchemy: Transform Your Life One Sip at a Time
The Mason Code: Leading in Unleadable Times
Petosiris and the Fifth Chamber of Thoth
The Ether Seed Within
The Parent of Tomorrow
Petosiris's Pyramid of Perpetual Wealth
Unlearn the World
Grimoire of the Hollow Tongue
Zodiac Weeds: Finding Your Strain Through the Stars
Aquarius Rises in the Bank
The Sugar God's Smile
The Skinclock Reversal: Biohacking the Face of Time
Debtburn: How to Obliterate What You Owe Forever
The Ice Cream Oracle: What Your Cone Says About Your Future
Silence Is Sovereignty: The Power of Being Unreadable
The Wind That Whispers Through Stone
Path of the Four Directions
Doctor Who: The Maestro's Symphony of Endings
Oxygen Grail: Breathing to Undo the Clock

Zodiacal Collapse: When Stars Devour Time
Teachings from the Red Sand Silence
Doctor Who: Omega – The Broken Equation
Memory Wipe Your Past: Start Over Like a MiB
Mitochondria Prime: Ignite the Core of Youth
A Nest of Roaches
Grub from the Galaxy: MiB Recipes You'll Never Forget
Whiskers of Power: Bastet's Guide to Inner Sovereignty
The Gift Must Cost Them: Negotiation Through Unequal Exchange
The Worm Guys' Wealth Code: Hustle Like an Alien
Bug Out: The Edgar Method for Ruthless Goal Setting
Weaving Life with Spiderwoman's Pattern
Doctor Who: The Rani's Renaissance
How to Get a Job (If You're a Puppygirl)
Speak Through Others: The Art of Proxy Power
T-Rex Your Trauma: Reclaim the Power of Your Primal Self
The Black Briefcase: How MiB Stay Wealthy in Silence
The Thirst Beyond Reason: Understanding Diabetes Insipidus From the Inside Out
Backwoods Witchcraft for Billionaires: The Pagan Path from Dirt Roads to Gold Roads
The Moonshine Grimoire: Fermented Spells for Abundance
The Nameless Geometry
The Wraith's Mixtape: Spellcasting with Songs of Sorrow
The Gallifreyan Gentleman: Silent Wealth, Sonic Confidence, and the Doctor's Code of Living
Sugar Water Confidence
Dino Totems: Spirit Guides from Earth's First Gods
Pumpkin Sigils & Ritual Smoke
The Hózhó Compass
The Distortus Discipline – Order from Inner Mutation
Witchcraft for the Cold-Blooded Soul

Moonlight Over the Blessingway

Water, Interrupted: When the Body Forgets How to Hold On

Deformed but Divine: Embracing Your Asymmetry

Hexes in the Henhouse: The Farm Witch's Guide to Power

The Reversed Flame: A Grimoire of Inverted Power

Salt, Cells, and Sanity: Reclaiming Balance with Diabetes Insipidus

King of the Broken: Crowning the Flawed Self

Moonlight Scars: Emo Moon Magick and the Art of Lunar Sorrow

Noose Spells: Magick of the Hanging Rope

The Goth Cathedral: Rituals of the Broken and Beautiful

The Cretaceous Codex: Dino Spirits and Fossil Magick

The Turkey Bones Ritual

Nine Lives of Manifestation: Unlocking Bastet's Reality Codes

Chaos Muscles: Building Strength from Twisted Pain

Emo Blood Magick: The Veins of Power

The 3AM Flood: Nighttime Urination, Sleep Loss, and the DI Spiral

The Silence Between the Stars

The Lemon Method: Sour Your Way to Success

Starlit Sovereign

The Rite of Twelve Gates: Walking the Gates of the Duat.

Cornbread and Conjure: Recipes for Riches and Rootwork

The Black Rose Rituals: Emo Love Spells and Obsession Magick

The Eternal Goodbye: Death Magick and Rebirth Rituals

Sinkrot: The Drain That Remembers

The Hybrid Mindset: Thinking Beyond Evolution

Bone Dry: Navigating Dehydration Before It Breaks You

Wreathcraft: Winter Sigils and Yuletide Spells

The Rite of Twelve Mouths

S'mores of the Damned: Haunted Recipes for Halloween Night

Rethink the Drink: A Beverage Survival Guide for DI Warriors

The Shadow Chord: Guitar Magick and Sonic

Malformed Yet Majestic: Leading When You Feel Wrong Inside

The Cursed Diary: Ink-Stained Spells of the Emo Soul

Anxiety Off Switch: Emergency Reset for a Fried Nervous System

The Energy Heist: How to Take Back Your Life from Drainers

Beyond the Bathroom: Rebuilding Your Social Life With DI

Coyote's Gift for Decision Makers

Ghoul-Goo: Spooky S'mores You'll Die For

Echoes in the Mirror: Scrying and Self-Destruction Magick

Thread and Thorn: Stitching Spells from Rural Cloth

The Mogwai Mind: Building Untouchable Wealth from Small Ideas

Be Your Own Guide: Trust Your Inner Compass

Hormones in Chaos: The Endocrine Puzzle of Diabetes Insipidus

ChronoCleanse: Detox Your Biological Timeline

The Limb You Hide Is the One That Saves You

Leaves, Bones, and Whisper Spells

The Dinosaur Mindset: Prehistoric Tactics for Modern Wealth

Clawing Back Control: A Bastet Method for Boundaries and Empowerment

Samhain Codes of the Forgotten

Orange Alchemy: The Autumnal Spellbook

Monster Within, Master Without

The Sigil That Sleeps

Hearthcraft: Yule Hearth Sigils and Winter Warmth Spells

Temple of the Purring Moon: Rituals from Bastet's Lineage
When the Earth Remembers Your Footsteps
Food for Mood: Eat to Heal Depression, Not Just Survive It
Witch of the Kudzu Vine: Southern Pagan Wealth Secrets
The Invisible Diagnosis: Advocating for Yourself With DI
The Coffin's Lullaby: Sleep Magick and Nightmares as Portals
Ashes of the Will: Rituals for Erasing the Self
The Fracture Rite: Shattering the Magickal Core
Funeral Candles: The Art of Emo Flame Magick
The Black Grimoire: A Blank Ritual for Writing in Absence
Phantom Thirst: A Halloween Survival Guide for Diabetes Insipidus
The Hollow Crown: Emo Royalty and Magick of the Outcast King
Sandpainting for the Soul
Falling Into Balance: Using the Extra Hour to Recalibrate Life
100 Southern Superstitions That Still Work
The DI Child: A Parent's Guide to Raising Hydrated, Happy Kids
The Jungle of Shame: Escaping the Hidden Lab of Doubt
The Witch's Toast: S'mores Spells and Creepy Confections
The Hoodoo Pantry: Spells from the Mason Jar
The Immortal Fortune: Secret Wealth Lessons from Captain Jack Harkness
The Specter's Embrace: Magick for Channeling Ghostly Lovers
Grateful Waters: A Thanksgiving Survival Guide for Diabetes Insipidus
The Seizure Gospel
Harvestbind: Autumn Sigils and Samhain Spells
Doctor Who: The Algorithmic Awakening
Silent Nights, Steady Waters: A Christmas Survival Guide for Diabetes Insipidus

The Extra Hour Effect: How One Hour Can Transform Everything

Blade Between the Breaths

Running with the Mountain Shadows

Echoes of the Failed Experiment – Becoming a Living Legacy

Swamp Witches & River Ghosts: Real Southern Hauntings

Cornbread Prophecies: Magical Recipes from a Southern Table

Doctor Who: The Signal in the Star

Bloomcraft: Spring Sigils and Equinox Enchantments

Vanisher: How to Disappear from the Internet Without Losing Your Life

The Ultimate Christmas Cookie Cookbook

The Unbreakable Parent: How to Mentally Survive Raising Kids in a Broken World

Time Debt: How to Reclaim the Hours You Didn't Know You Lost

One Month, One Million: Unconventional Cash Creation Tactics

Doctor Who: The Cyber Conversion Protocol

Black Friday Frenzy: The Art of Finding Hidden Online Deals

The Grimoire Buried Under the Apple Tree

Digital Couponing Masterclass: Your Step-by-Step Guide to Black Friday Savings

The Fire Inside the Flint

Shadows on the Ceiling: The Emo Guide to Astral Magick

The Bone-Eaters Beneath Us

Black Friday Bundle Blueprint: Creating Irresistible Product Packages for Maximum Sales

Thirteen Nights of Unbinding

Doctor Who: Engines of Influence

Pumpkin Spice Alchemy: Recipes of Fire and Frost

When Raptor Met Rexy: Prehistoric Lessons in Wild Romance

Oblivion's Candle: Burn the Path Behind You

Campfire Curses and Chocolate: A Halloween S'mores Grimoire

The Wallet That Wasn't Mine: Breaking Free from Inherited Scarcity

The Cola Zodiac: What Your Fizz Says About Your Fate

Frostfire Fortune: Unlocking Winter's Hidden Prosperity

Signal Jamming: Detox Your Brain from Info Overload

The Dust of the Forgotten Rite

The Golden Cat Sigils: Drawing Power in Bastet's Name

Mud Magick: The Prosperity of Getting Dirty

Savory Spicefall: Beyond the Pumpkin Pie

Pumpkin Spice Apothecary Kitchen

The Pumpkin Spice Economy: Turning Trends into Billions

The Ember Veil: 13 Nights of Fire Magick

Financial Freeze: When Earning Triggers Panic

The Gingerbread Alchemist: Sweet Recipes with a Twist

Biosynth Power: Programming Yourself from Scratch

Echoes from the Talking Circle

Truffle Alchemy: Fungus of Fortune

Spores of Power: The Truffle Witch's Handbook

Doctor Who: The Tower That Speaks

The Mycelium Veil: Truffle Magick Unbound

Broke But Ashamed: Healing the Shame Wound of Debt

The Evergreen Mind: Growth Through Winter Stillness

The Black Veil Truffle Rite

The Voice Beneath Symbols

Witchlight on the Bayou: Swamp Spells for Sovereignty

I Grew Up Poor and Now I Sabotage My Success

The Lantern of Hollow Souls

Shutdown Survival: A Citizen's Guide to Thriving When Government Stops

When Abundance Feels Like a Threat: Healing the Hidden Fears of Enough

The Scarecrow Grimoire

Owls of the October Veil

Candlewax and Curses: A Halloween Spellbook

Excavating the Inner Fossil – Transforming Fossilized Thoughtforms into Tools of Power

The Yule Witch's Spellbook: Magick for the Holiday Season

Haunted Christmas: Ghost Stories for Winter Nights

The Christmas Survival Guide: Thriving Through the Chaos

The Bone Orchard Rites

Haunted Commerce: The Ghost in the Marketplace

When Money Triggers the Inner Child

Silent Night with the Silence: A Christmas Thriller

The Lightning Crown: Living and Leading Through Seizures

TARDIS Tidings: Festive Stories from the Whoniverse

Autumn Reset: Slowing Down Without Falling Behind

The Trillion Dollar Soul: Rewriting the Currency of Reality

Truffle Eclipse Magick

Micro-Manifestations: Quick Magick That Works

5-Minute Rituals for Busy Witches

The Marshmallow Massacre: Halloween Treats with a Sinister Twist

Blood and Blackberry Thorns

Magickal Mornings: Rituals for a Blessed Christmas Day

Embers of the All-Hallows Fire

The Pumpkin Market Collapse

The Hour You Gained: Transforming Time Into Power

The Chamber Must Be Sealed: Mastering the Power of Controlled Access

The Cursed Manuscript of Petosiris

The Festive Hearth: Creating Holiday Traditions
Darkness Rising: Thriving as Nights Grow Longer
Harvesting Time: Turning the Year's End Into Your New Beginning
Petosiris and the 13th Zodiac Key
Wagewound: When Paychecks Become Identity Prisons
Walls That Watch
The Silent Feast: Rituals of Power in the Longest Night
The Distortus Legacy : Becoming a Deformed King in a Perfect World
The Hollow Masks
The Gratitude Furnace: Forging Gold from Thanks
Feast of Inner Gold: Eating for Energy and Enlightenment
Haunted Commerce: The Season of Spending Spirits
Fear Bonds: How Panic Creates Profit
Black Friday E-Commerce Playbook: Sales Tactics to Skyrocket Your Holiday Revenue
Budgeting for Black Friday: A Holiday Savings Planner
Haunting the Harvest Moon
The Warrior's Water: Emergency Preparedness for People With DI
The First Sip of the Year: A New Year's Survival Guide for Diabetes Insipidus
Doctor Who: The Thirteenth Node
The Unseen Struggle: Mental Health, Anxiety, and Chronic Thirst
The Hearth's Hidden Ledger: Counting Energies as Currency
The Gift Alchemist: Turning Any Offering Into Gold
The Papyrus of the Bound Spirit
The Magick of Leftovers: Transmutation in the Fridge
Frost and Fortune: Christmas Wealthcraft for the Modern Magus
Last-Minute Gifts: Creative Ideas on a Budget

10 Secrets to Surviving Holiday Crowds
The Witch's Dow Jones
The Witches' Graveyard Shift
Pumpkin Sigils: Carving Rites for Midnight Power
The Secret Shopper's Black Friday Guide: How to Get Early Access and VIP Deals
Fever in the Foundation
The Neuralyzer Reset: Reprogram Your Morning Routine
Lightning Lessons of the White Painted Woman
The Enchanted Snowflake
The Magic Sip: Surviving Disney Parks with Diabetes Insipidus
The One Who Draws Through You
Santa's Secrets: A Magical Holiday Planner
Silent Bells, Loud Miracles: Self-Help for the Season of Stillness
The Sugar Spell Codex: Confectionary Magick of Christmas
Autumn Hexcraft: Fallen Leaves, Fallen Barriers
Sleep Like a Fortress: Build a Life Where Insomnia Can't Survive
Nowhere Was Ever Home
Christmas Under the Stars: A Celestial Holiday Guide
Rentproof: How to Never Be Evicted Again
Workless: Escape the 9-5 Without Being Broke
The Gilded Gift: A Wealth Altar for Christmas Morning
The Black Friday Grimoire
The Hollowing: Ceremonies of Spiritual Collapse
Doctor Who: The Nameless Signal
Where the Eagle Hides His Courage
The Dwarf Tyrant's Ascent: Claiming Power in a World of Giants
The Currency of the Dead: Trading with Spectral Bankers
The Icebound Witch: Survival and Magick in the Cold

The Emergency Money Mind: Constant Crisis, Zero Calm

Thirst & Roses: A Valentine's Survival Guide for Diabetes Insipidus

Springing Into Clarity: Mastering the Energy Shift of Daylight Saving

Speed of the Nanotyrant: Agile Strategies for Life's Hunt

The 90-Day Reset: A Science-Backed Guide to Reinvent Yourself Before the New Year

The Coil of Thorns

Timegates Unleashed

Dopamine Fasting 2.0: Rewiring Your Brain in a World of Overstimulation

The Nanotyrannus Mutation: Embracing Your Differentiated Form

Unwritten January: How to Use the Blank Page of the Year to Re-Author Your Life

Feast of the Forgotten Spirits: Ancestor Magick for the Holidays

The Burnout Codex: A System for Thriving Beyond Stress

I Don't Deserve to Have Money

When the King Doesn't See You: The Shadow Predator's Guide

The Reset Ritual :A Guide to Shedding Last Year's Weight—Emotional and Physical—by Spring Cleaning Your Soul

Calendar Alchemy: Learn to Bend Time and Productivity around Your Natural Rhythms

The Mirror Contract: A One-Sentence Agreement with Yourself that Unlocks Real Change

The Nile Formula: Sacred Flow for Millionaire Minds

Forward Momentum: Productivity Rituals for the Lost Hour

Harvest Gold: Wealth Magick of Pumpkin Spice Commerce

The Magick of Christmas Lights: Illuminating Holiday Rituals

Cranberry Crown: Royal Self-Worth through Ritual Meals

Petosiris and the Worms of the Feathered Throne

The Evergreen Equation: Self-Help for Sustained Growth

The Rain Will Wash Us Away: Emo Weather Magick

Snowlight Shadows: Magick Under Frozen Stars

Doctor Who: Merger of Empires

The Light Within the Feast: Magickal Wealth of Yuletide Flame

Momentum Machines: Small Habits Designed to Snowball into Unstoppable Forward Motion

Calm Spells: Magickal Solutions for Anxiety Relief

Santa's Final List: The Naughty Never Leave

The Mystic's Guide to Banishing Worry

The Silence Dividend: Turning Quiet Mornings into Compounding Growth All Year

Charmed Stillness: Rituals to Ease the Mind

Blood Spiral Ascension

The Vanishing Heart Invocation

Crystal Calm: Harnessing Stones for Anxiety

The Nano Tyrant Code: Strength in the Small Predator

The Energy Ledger: Accounting Methods for Vitality, Not Just Money

Snowglobe Mindset: Shake Up Your Thoughts, Settle Into Peace

The Weight of the Feather: Anubis's Codes for Soul Balance

Pocket Peppermint Power: Tiny Rituals for Big Holiday Energy

Shadowkeeper of the Golden Jackal: Anubis's Path to Energetic Protection

The Witch's Breath: Anxiety Relief Through Magickal Breathing

The Tiny Ember: Pocket Motivation for Cold Days

Stocking Sorcery: Mini Spells for Holiday Luck and Prosperity

Warm Hands, Steady Heart: Micro Grounding for Winter Anxiety

The Jackal's Lantern: Guide-Lights for Walking the Dark Path

Anubis's Silent Steps: Rituals for Stealth, Peace & Emotional Quiet

The Bonewake Protocol

Extinction-Proof: How to Outlive Trends, Trauma, and Time

The Fourth Doctor: The Eccentric Wanderer

The Second Doctor: Chaos and Charm in the TARDIS (Patrick Troughton, 1966–1969)

The Third Doctor: Earthbound Defender of Time (Jon Pertwee, 1970–1974)

The First Doctor: Genesis of the Time Lord (William Hartnell, 1963–1966)

The Fourth Doctor: The Eccentric Wanderer ***(Tom Baker, 1974–1981)***

The Fifth Doctor: Elegance and Empathy (Peter Davison, 1982–1984)

The Sixth Doctor: A Kaleidoscope of Conflict (Colin Baker, 1984–1986)

The Seventh Doctor: The Strategist of Shadows (Sylvester McCoy, 1987–1989)

The Eighth Doctor: A Time Lord's Renaissance (Paul McGann, 1996)

The War Doctor: A Time Lord's Burden (John Hurt, 2013)

The Ninth Doctor: The Healer of Worlds ***(Christopher Eccleston, 2005)***

The Tenth Doctor: The Lonely Hero (David Tennant, 2005–2010)

The Eleventh Doctor: The Madman in a Box (Matt Smith, 2010–2013)

The Twelfth Doctor: The Rebel with a Cause (Peter Capaldi, 2013–2017)

The Thirteenth Doctor: Breaking the Mold
(Jodie Whittaker, 2017–2022)

The Fourteenth Doctor: A New Beginning (David Tennant, 2022–2023)

The Fifteenth Doctor: Rewriting the Stars
(Ncuti Gatwa, 2023–2025)

Santa's Shortcut to Success: Micro Habits for a Better New Year

The Midnight Cocoa Manifesto: Comfort Rituals for Hard Nights

Why I Can't Save: Trauma Blocks to Financial Planning

Dino Brain, Mega Goals: Rewire Yourself for Savage Success.

Jurassic Profit: Unearth Your Inner Millionaire Fossil

Scales & Softness: Dating with Dino Heart

Carnotaurus Dreams.

Red Willow Thinking.

Reindeer Resilience: How to Keep Going When You're Exhausted

Candlewick Courage: Lighting Strength in Dark Seasons.

Elf-Mode Focus: Fast Attention Fixes for Busy Seasons

Futureproof Feelings: Emotional Skill-Building for Resilience No Matter What the New Year Brings

The 90-Day Rewire: Transform Your Neural Pathways Before Spring Blooms

Jolly Rich: Christmas Micro-Money Magick for Fast Prosperity.

Gingerbread Gratitude: Mini Practices for a Happier Holiday

Trauma-Spending: When Money Becomes a Drug

Goal Skeletons: Build Minimalist Frameworks for Resolutions That Last

The Snarl Strategy: Growling Back at a World That Silenced You

The Hourglass Reset: Reclaiming What the Clock Took

Yule Claw: Dino Rites of Light in the Darkness

Sacred Circles: Grounding Rituals for Anxious Souls

Clockstopper's Gut: Rebuilding the Core of Time

Winterfire Drive: Harness the Cold Season's Stillness to Ignite Deep Motivation

The 5-Minute Productivity Hack: Small Steps to Big Results

Light Ascending: A Self-Help Guide to Longer Days

Inner Economy: Trade Self-Doubt for Confidence Like a High-Value Currency

Simple Success: Decluttering Your Life for Better Results

The Resilient Mind: Thriving in Tough Times

The 2026 Playbook: Mastering the Year Ahead

The Spring Sleep Solution: Conquering Fatigue After Time Change.

The Hormonal Compass: Navigate Back to Your Youth

Golden Vision: Eating for Your Eye Color with the Power of Ghee

Lionhearted Love: Strength in Relationships

MiB Mindset: Think Like a Cosmic Agent

The Ladder of Small Wins: Climb Out of Stagnation by Stacking Micro-Victories

The Momentum Hour: Gaining More in Less Time.

The Year of You: A Self-Help Blueprint for Unapologetic Self-Ownership

The Dust That Watches You Back.

The Astral Parent

Shadow of the King: The Nanotyrannus Parable

Tiny Tidings of Triumph: Small Wins That Change Your Life

Dwarf Tyrant Rising: When You're the One They Overlook

The Bank Account Mirror: Healing How You See Yourself Through Money

Cretaceous Black

When Love Costs Too Much: Romantic Triggers and Financial Wounds

Dream-Eater's Guide to Wealth

Unzipped Reality: The Jacket That Opens Portals

The Power of No: How to Set Boundaries and Get Rich

Keeper of the Desert Veil: Anubis's Teachings on Illusion & Truth

Redacted Stargates: Stories the SGC Buried

The Clock That Dripped Time

Doctor Who: The Silent Acquisition

Hairline Manifestation: Unlocking Power at the Edge of Thought

Cash-Eater Crickets: How Insects Predict Economic Collapse

Dead Pet Whisperer: Grief Alchemy from the Other Side

The Love Algorithm Is Broken: Hack Romance Before It Hacks You

The Rite of the 8-Limbed Seal

Melt the Moon: A Fire Ritual to Reshape Emotion

Venomous Miracles: Healing Through the Poison Path

Wealth Without Water: The Post-Aquatic Rich Life

The Butterfly Betrayal: When Change Turns on You

The Quiet Upgrade: How Humans Are Secretly Rebuilding Themselves Without Asking Permission

Nobody Taught Us This: The Missing Human Manual for Money, Energy, and Self-Respect

You Were Never Broken: Why Most People Are Reacting Normally to an Unstable World

After the Noise Ends: How Humans Reset When the World Finally Goes Quiet

The Month That Tells the Truth: Why January Reveals What the Rest of the Year Hides

Tremors Party Unleashed: The Ultimate Guide to a Graboids Birthday Bash

Cold Start Human: Rebooting Motivation Without Forcing Momentum

The Year that doesn't start until they say

Love Without Performance: What Connection Looks Like When No One Is Watching

February Is a Mirror: What Love Exposes About You

How We Learned Love Wrong: Uninstalling Cultural Myths About Connection

You Are Not Too Much: Why Needing Love Is Not a Flaw

The Crooked Fence Covenant: Backwoods Boundaries and Witch Wealth

The Day That Keeps Repeating: Why Your Life Feels Stuck—and How to Shift It Gently

Nothing Changes Until Something Softens: Escaping Repetition Without Violence to Yourself

Same Life, Different Ending: How Tiny Choices Rewrite Repetition

The Loop Isn't Punishment: Why You're Being Asked to Learn, Not Suffer

Panic at the Register: Retail Anxiety and Public Shame

The Secret Formula to Becoming an Influencer in 90 Days

The New Rich: How to Retire by 35

Digital Nomad Secrets: How to Travel the World and Make Millions

Burn Your Waiting Room: Escape the Delay Spiral

Strapped for Pleasure: A Complete Guide to Pegging and Strap-On Play

Locked in Desire: A Guide to Chastity Play and Intimate Control

Burrowing into History: Groundhog Day Through the Ages

The Shadow Forecast: The Science of Groundhog Day

Choice Cascades: How One Decision in January Sets Ripples for the Whole Year

The Anti-Anxiety Blueprint: Mastering Fear and Stress for Success

The Ancestral Path of the Jackal Priest

Winterborn Titans: Giants of Ice and Stone

The Extinction Spire

The Emotion That Made Me Millions

Delete Their Voice: Become Unreachable

The Frostbound Mysteries: Mythical Beings of January's Chill

The Roar Within: Unlocking Your Potential

From Burrow to Sky: Groundhog Day Explained

The Boogey Book: Festive Ward-Off Edition

Fooled Ya! The Psychology Behind Great Pranks

April Fools' Alchemy: Transforming Everyday Items into Pranks

Anchor Habits: Root Yourself in Unshakable Routines That Endure Seasonal Change

Emerald Waters: A St. Patrick's Day Survival Guide for Diabetes Insipidus

The Groundhog's Legacy: Myths, Legends, and Facts

Six Weeks of Mystery: The Truth Behind Groundhog Day

The Upgrade Mind: Tech-Like Patches and Updates for Your Mental Operating System

Moon Blood, Star Flesh: Embracing Your Hybrid Nature

Groundhog Lore and Legend: A Complete Guide

You Are the Lie They Can't Kill

Download a Different Reality

The Quiet Advantage: Winning Without Announcing Yourself

A Year of Gratitude: Unlocking Joy

Touch Grass: A Pagan Reset for a Burned-Out Digital World
Cold Start Wealth: Building Financial Power from a Standing Still Point
Astrology Without Fate: Using Cycles Without Surrendering Control
The Future is Remote: Work Less, Earn More, Live Anywhere
Harvest of Silence
The Algorithm Knows Your Name
April Fools' Day for Introverts
Soft Power Systems: Influence That Doesn't Exhaust You
Practical Magick for Real Life: Focus, Intent, and Follow-Through
January Is a Lie: Designing Momentum Without the Calendar
Universal Flow: Managing DI in High-Energy Theme Parks
Electric Allure: Exploring Erotic Electro-Play
The Masked Embrace: Exploring Sensory Deprivation
The Ultimate April Fools' Survival Guide
Splashproof Survival: Waterparks & Wave Pools with DI
Agile Predator, Still King: Crafting Your Speed in a World That Celebrates Size
The Shadow Feast: Groundhog Day's Sinister Side
The Bug's Business Model
Edge of Bliss: Mastering the Art of Tease and Denial
Midnight Alchemy: Rituals for Transformation Between the Old Year and the New
Punxsutawney Bloodlines: A Groundhog Day Horror
The Burrower: Groundhog Day's Darkest Secrets
Buried Alive: A Groundhog Day Horror Story
Blood Moon Markets: The Witch's Guide to Wealth Magick
The Groundhog's Shadow: What It Means for the World
Seasonal Shadows: The Groundhog Day Phenomenon
The Shadow's Curse: A Groundhog Day Horror Tale
Punxsutawney Revealed: A Guide to Groundhog Day

Safari Hydration: Zoo & Wildlife Park Survival for DI
The Foolproof Prank Planner
Latex Lust: Embracing Fetish Fashion is a sophisticated
Whip & Whisper: The Dynamics of Impact Play
The Shadow Burrow Chronicles: Horror Beneath the Ground
Frozen Shadows: A Groundhog Day Thriller
The Groundhog's Revenge: A February Nightmare
Burrow of the Damned
Everyday Enchantment: Magickal Practices for Modern Living
Budget Bliss: The Easy Path to Financial Freedom
Six More Weeks of Terror
The Oxygen Debt
The Ice Veil: Mystical Beasts of January's Shadows
Roots That Remember
Polar Myths: Creatures of the Icy Abyss
The Marginalia Covenant
AI and the Occult: Digital Spirits, Sigils, and Cyber-Witchcraft
Roleplay Realms: Crafting Fantasies and Scenes
The Last Clean River
Lover in the Shadows: A Groundhog Day Tale
Buried Hearts: A Groundhog Day Gothic Romance
Anubis Wept for Petosiris
The Lantern Knows Your Name
Rituals of the Last Shadow
The Bell That Rings for No One
Shadows of Love and Death
The Groundhog's Bride: A Dark Valentine's Tale
Frozen Kisses: A Horror Romance for Groundhog Day
The Creative Spark: Igniting Your Passion Projects
From Cub to King: A Journey of Transformation
Six Weeks to Midnight: A Groundhog Day Romance
Tide of the Unclean

Burrow of Desire: A Groundhog Day Paranormal Romance

The Shadow Magick Almanac: Harnessing Groundhog Day Energies

www.ingramcontent.com/pod-product-compliance
Lightning Source LLC
LaVergne TN
LVHW022009200926
848481LV00007B/2308
* 9 7 9 8 2 9 5 5 6 5 7 1 7 *